MARTIAL ARTS

KARATE

Harry Cook (fourth dan) is the chief instructor of the Seijnhai Karate-Do Association.
The models are Katy Cook (first dan) and Josh Learman (first dan).

Please visit our web site at: **www.garethstevens.com**
For a free color catalog describing Gareth Stevens Publishing's
list of high-quality books and multimedia programs,
call 1-800-542-2595 (USA) or 1-800-387-3178 (Canada).
Gareth Stevens Publishing's fax: (414) 332-3567.

Library of Congress Cataloging-in-Publication Data

Cook, Harry.
    Karate / Harry Cook. — North American ed.
       p. cm. — (Martial arts)
    Includes bibliographical references and index.
    ISBN 0-8368-4193-X (lib. bdg.)
    1. Karate—Juvenile literature. I. Title. II. Martial arts (Milwaukee, Wis.)
    GV1114.3.C66   2004
    796.815'3—dc22   2004045209

This North American edition first published in 2005 by
Gareth Stevens Publishing
A World Almanac Education Group Company
330 West Olive Street, Suite 100
Milwaukee, WI 53212 USA

Original edition © 2003 by David West Children's Books. First published in Great Britain
in 2003 by Raintree, Halley Court, Jordan Hill, Oxford OX2 8EJ, part of Harcourt Education.
Raintree is a registered trademark of Harcourt Education Ltd. This U.S. edition © 2005 by
Gareth Stevens, Inc. Additional end matter © 2005 by Gareth Stevens, Inc.

Photographer: Sylvio Dokov
David West editor: Gail Bushnell
David West designer: Gary Jeffrey
Gareth Stevens editor: Alan Wachtel
Gareth Stevens designer: Steve Schraenkler
Gareth Stevens art direction: Tammy West
Gareth Stevens production: Jessica Morris

Photo Credits:
Abbreviations: (t) top, (m) middle, (b) bottom, (r) right, (l) left, (c) center

All photos by Sylvio Dokov except Getty Images: 6(tr), 6(br). Jed Jacobsohn: front cover,
11(t), 12(t), 13(t), 16(t), 21(tl), 27(mr). Matthew Stockman: 26(bl).

Sylvio Dokov was born in Sofia, Bulgaria. For the past two decades, he has been one of Europe's leading martial arts
photographers. Sylvio works from his own studio in Telford, Shropshire.

Printed in the United States of America

1 2 3 4 5 6 7 8 9 08 07 06 05 04

MARTIAL ARTS

KARATE

Harry Cook

GARETH**STEVENS**
GS
PUBLISHING
A World Almanac Education Group Company

CONTENTS

INTRODUCTION

Martial arts are ways of learning to defend yourself and develop physical and mental discipline. Many of them are also international competitive sports. Experts agree that the only way to really learn a martial art is to train with a qualified teacher.

This book introduces some of the basic techniques of karate, a popular martial art that is practiced in many different styles. Read the text carefully and look closely at the pictures to see how to do some basic karate moves.

HISTORY

The history of karate begins in China, where the most famous center of martial arts was located in the Shaolin Temple in Henan Province. Chinese martial arts spread to the island of Okinawa and blended with Okinawan martial arts to produce karate. The word *karate* originally meant "China hand."

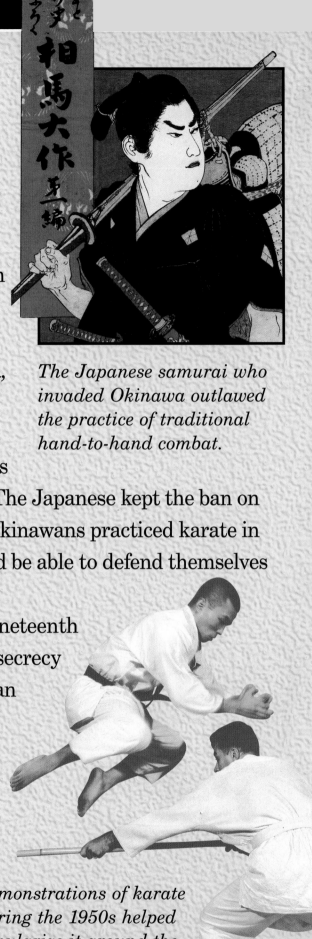

The Japanese samurai who invaded Okinawa outlawed the practice of traditional hand-to-hand combat.

In 1609, Japanese samurai from Satsuma, who were equipped with guns, conquered Okinawa, where weapons had long been banned. The Japanese kept the ban on weapons in force. The Okinawans practiced karate in secret so that they would be able to defend themselves against the conquerors.

Gichin Funakoshi

By the end of the nineteenth century, the traditional secrecy surrounding karate began to disappear. In 1922, an Okinawan teacher named Gichin Funakoshi opened a karate *dojo*, or training hall, in Tokyo, Japan. In the 1930s, the characters used to write "China hand" were changed to those that mean "empty hand," although they were still pronounced as "karate."

Demonstrations of karate during the 1950s helped popularize it around the world as a sport.

CLOTHING AND ETIQUETTE

Before the development of the modern karate uniform, karate students on Okinawa wore a *fundoshi,* or loincloth. When karate was taken to Japan in 1922, a lighter-weight version of the uniform used in judo was developed for karate training.

The karate uniform consists of a jacket and pants, both of which are usually made of strong, white, cotton cloth and are fastened by strings at the waist and the hips.

BELTS
Karate students wear colored belts that indicate their ranks. Below is a sample of a karate ranking system. Higher ranks are awarded for accomplishments in technique, sparring, and understanding of karate.

unranked
9th *kyu*
8th *kyu*
7th *kyu*
6th *kyu*
5th *kyu*
4th *kyu*
3rd *kyu*
2nd *kyu*
1st *kyu*
dan ranks

1   2

3   4

HOW TO TIE THE BELT
1. Place the center of the belt across your stomach.
2. Wrap the belt around your back and bring the ends around to the front.
3. Cross the right end of the belt over the left end and under both layers of cloth.
4. Tie a square knot.

Students bow at the beginning and end of karate classes. Bowing shows respect. Students also bow to each other when training.

A karate class usually starts with warm-up exercises. Students stretch the upper body, back, and legs. Push-ups, sit-ups, and squats build strength and stamina.

KARATE STANCES

Stances (*tachi*) are the foundations of karate. Stances are used to move toward your opponent for an attack, move away when your opponent attacks you, protect your body from attacks, and provide a solid base for punching, kicking, and blocking.

FRONT STANCE (*zenkutsu dachi*)

1. Place one leg ahead of the other, bending the knee of the front leg until the shin is vertical. Straighten the back leg with the knee and ankle joint held firmly, as if the edge of the foot was pushing into the ground. Point the toes of the rear foot forward and keep the back straight.

2. To shift into a front stance on the opposite side, move the rear leg forward in a slight curve, as if protecting the groin. Do not bend forward or sideways, and keep the shoulders relaxed. Keep the knees slightly bent. Step forward into a front stance.

CAUTION!

Karate training can be dangerous. If you want to learn karate, you must take lessons from a qualified karate teacher. The information in this book cannot take the place of a qualified teacher. Do not practice any of the techniques in this book in any way that might injure yourself or another person.

1

2

BACK STANCE
(kokutsu dachi)

Moving your weight backward can unbalance an opponent who has grabbed your lapels or throat.

1. Place one leg ahead of the other, bend both knees, and shift your weight to the rear foot. Place the heel of the front foot at a right angle to the rear foot. The edge of the rear foot should push into the ground.

2. To shift sides, move the back foot forward until the knees pass each other.

3. Step forward into the next back stance. Keep the back straight and the shoulders relaxed.

STRADDLE STANCE
(kiba dachi)

Kiba dachi is used to position yourself sideways to an opponent. This stance is important when defending against attacks and also as the ready position when practicing side kicks.

1. Spread the feet about two shoulder widths apart, keeping them parallel to each other. Push the outer edges of the feet into the floor. Allow the knees to bend, creating a bow shape with the legs.

2. To move forward, bring the rear foot across the front foot. Do not lean forward.

3. Step into the next *kiba dachi*.

STANDING PUNCH
(choku zuki)

The standing punch is the most basic karate punch. Make sure the returning hand feels as if you have grabbed and pulled an opponent into the punch.

To correctly make a fist, open the hand flat. Fold back the fingers at the knuckles and then roll up the fingers tightly. Bind the fingers with the thumb. When striking a target, hit with the first two knuckles only.

1. Stand with the feet shoulder-width apart. Extend one hand to the front and place the other hand on the hip, with the palm up.

2. Move the hand on the hip to the front while pulling the extended arm back toward the hip position.

3. Pull the extended arm down to the hip while punching with the opposite fist, twisting the hips to help generate power for the punch.

LUNGE PUNCH
(oi zuki)

The lunge punch is the basic stepping punch in most styles of karate. This punch is usually practiced in a front stance, or *zenkutsu dachi*, but it is also practiced in other basic stances.

The fighter on the right scores a point by driving a strong basic punch forward.

1

2

3

1. Stand in a front stance and extend the front hand with the fist tightly clenched.

2. Move the back foot forward until the knees and ankles are together.

3. Step forward and punch with the fist on the same side that is moving forward.

REVERSE PUNCH
(gyaku zuki)

The reverse punch, or *gyaku zuki*, is like the lunge punch, except the punch comes from the opposite side of the body. If the right leg is forward, punch with the left fist, and vice versa.

The fighter on the right uses a fast hip rotation to drive a punch to its target.

1

2

3

1. Stand in a front stance and extend the arm on the side opposite the front leg.

2. Move the back foot forward until the knees and ankles are together.

3. Continue to step forward with the same leg and punch from the side opposite that leg.

JAB PUNCH
(kizami zuki)

Kizami zuki is like a boxing jab. When practicing the jab punch with a partner, use control to avoid hitting your partner's face.

These fighters are blocking and using correct distance to protect themselves against each other's attack.

1

2

1. Stand in a front stance.

2. Push forward on the front foot while simultaneously punching with the front fist. Do not pull the punching hand backward while pushing the body forward. Concentrate on driving strongly forward. Driving forward adds power to the punch and helps to achieve the correct distance.

RISING BLOCK
(age uke)

1

In karate, blocks are used for defense. Good blocking skills are very important. Gichin Funakoshi taught that "there is no first attack in karate."

Using age uke, *it is possible to deflect a powerful kick.*

OUTSIDE BLOCK
(soto uke)

1

In basic karate, the outside block is commonly used against a punch. In more advanced karate, this technique also is used to break a grip, such as a grab of the lapels, or a strangle.

While practicing, karate students must never use a full-power outside block on a partner's elbow joint because it will badly hurt the partner's elbow.

2

3

1. Stand in a front stance with the front arm held up, as if protecting the head.

2. Move the front foot back until the knees and ankles are together.

3. Step back with the same leg and move the opposite arm upward and across the face. Twist the hips while moving the arm up to increase the power of the block.

2

3

1. Stand in a front stance, holding the forward arm in front of the chest.

2. While moving the front foot backward, extend the front arm and raise the opposite forearm to block.

3. Twisting the hips and forearm, move the blocking forearm across the chest, as if deflecting a punch. Keep a strong stance.

INSIDE BLOCK
(uchi uke)

This block is generally used to defend the chest and stomach area. Move the forearm in an outward curve from the hip or waist to perform *uchi uke*.

The fighter on the right is using gedan barai *to block a roundhouse kick.*

1 **2** **3**

1. Stand in a front stance, holding the front arm with the palm upward and the elbow bent.

2. While moving the front foot back and past the opposite foot, straighten the front arm and place the opposite arm and hand, palm down, across the chest.

3. Step back into a front stance, rotating the forearm up and out from the chest, as if deflecting a punch.

DOWN BLOCK
(gedan barai)

Perform *gedan barai* by moving the forearm downward, as if to stop a kick aimed at the stomach. In general, this block should be used with a slight side step to avoid taking the full power of a kick on the arm.

1. Stand in a front stance with the front arm held downward, fist clenched.

2. While moving the front foot back and past the opposite foot, place the fist of the rear hand on the opposite shoulder.

3. Step back into a front stance, moving the blocking hand down in a smooth curve to block an attack.

KNIFEHAND BLOCK
(shuto uke)

The knifehand block is often the first open-hand block taught to beginners. It is usually practiced in back stance. The movement of body weight over the rear leg can be used to unbalance an attacker who may have grabbed your wrist or clothing.

1. Stand in a back stance with the blocking hand (the back hand) across the chest.

2. Move the front foot back and the blocking hand to the opposite shoulder, then straighten the front hand.

3. Step into a back stance, moving the blocking hand across the body to block an attack.

BACK FIST
(uraken)

To perform *uraken,* snap the fist in a curved motion at a target, using the elbow like a hinge. Twisting the hips can give extra speed.

1

1. Point the elbow at the target with the closed fist touching the chest, the palm down.

2. Moving the fist in a curve, hit the target with the knuckles. Some instructors say that the wrist should curve in slightly just before the hand strikes the target.

2

3. Snap the fist back to the ready position. Do not jerk the elbow joint. Jerking the elbow can injure the arm.

3

One good way to develop back-fist speed is to try hitting a piece of paper that has been dropped by a training partner.

ELBOW
(empi or hiji)

The elbow strike is used when close to an opponent. Hit with the point of the elbow. Twist the hips to add speed.

The elbow (*yoko empi*) is used to strike to the side. An upward elbow strike (*age empi*) is used to attack an opponent's jaw. A rear elbow strike (*ushiro empi*) is used when an attacker grabs you from behind.

yoko empi

ushiro empi

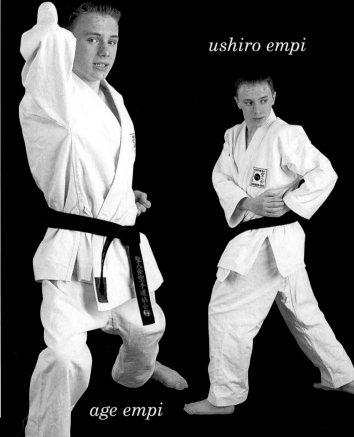

age empi

FRONT KICK
(mae geri)

The front kick is the most direct kick in karate. Also known as *mae geri,* this kick is a very powerful technique. It is used mainly to attack the stomach or groin.

1. Stand in a front stance.

2. Lift the knee of the kicking leg as high as possible.

3. Kick the lower part of the leg forward. Curl back the toes so the ball of the foot hits the target. Push the hips and stomach forward as the kick hits.

4. Pull the kick back quickly to prevent the leg from being caught. It is important to keep the knee of the supporting leg slightly bent and the foot flat.

1   2   3   4

Practice the front kick by kicking over a karate belt stretched across two chairs. If the knee is too low, the toes will hit the belt. Keep the knee high to stop the leg from swinging upward instead of driving directly to the target.

SIDE KICKS
(yoko geri)

Side kicks use the edge of the foot *(sokuto)* to strike a target. These kicks are very powerful. Karate uses two basic side kicks: the side thrust kick (*yoko geri kekomi*) and the side snap kick (*yoko geri keage*).

**SIDE THRUST KICK
*(yoko geri kekomi)***

1. Stand in a straddle stance (*kiba dachi*).

2. Move the rear foot forward and step over the front of the supporting leg.

3. Lift the knee of the kicking leg as high as possible, keeping the edge of the foot parallel to the floor.

4. Drive the foot in a straight line to the target. Twist the hips and the supporting leg to add power to the kick.

5. Pull the kicking foot back close to the supporting leg.

6. Step forward into *kiba dachi*.

In April 1979, Scientific American *published an article saying that "in a well placed side kick the foot can withstand roughly 2,000 times more force than concrete can."*

SIDE SNAP KICK
(yoko geri keage)

1. Stand in a straddle stance (*kiba dachi*).

2. Move the rear foot forward and step over the front of the supporting leg.

3. Lift the knee of the kicking leg as high as possible, keeping the edge of the foot parallel to the floor.

4. Snap the foot in a rising curve to the target.

5. Pull the kicking foot back close to the supporting leg and step forward into *kiba dachi*.

Practice the side thrust kick while holding onto a chair for balance. Imagine the kick moving through a target, not just touching it.

BACK KICK
(ushiro geri)

The back kick is a powerful technique that involves the strong leg and hip muscles. It is used when attacked from behind.

Use a target, such as a rolled up newspaper, to help develop an accurate back kick.

1. Stand in a front stance.

2. Twist the body around, turning the head to look at the target.

3. Lift the knee of the kicking leg and thrust the leg backward, fully extending it in a straight line. Keep the toes pointing toward the ground and strike the target with the heel.

4. Pull the leg back, keeping your eyes on the target.

1

ROUNDHOUSE KICK
(mawashi geri)

Perform *mawashi geri* like a curving punch with the leg. Lift the knee high, then move it in a curve toward the target.

Practice with a partner to improve the balance and extension of the roundhouse kick.

1. Stand in a front stance.

2. Lift the kicking leg and point the knee at the target.

3. Snap the leg to full extension. Strike with the instep while twisting the hips and the supporting ankle.

4. Pull the leg back.

1

2   **3**   **4**

2   **3**   **4**

FORMS
(kata)

Kata, or forms, are fixed sequences of karate blocks, punches, kicks, strikes, throws, and locks. Karate uses many *kata.* Practicing *kata* is good exercise and develops good technique. *Kata* are often called "the heart of karate."

Tsuguo Sakumoto has won many world kata *competitions.*

KIHON KATA

Kihon kata was developed in the late 1930s. These photos show only part of the *kata.* For steps fourteen through twenty-two, repeat steps three through eleven. After step twenty-two, repeat steps two through six to finish the *kata.*

1. *Yoi* (ready). Stand with fists gripped tightly in front of you.

2. Step into a left down block.

3. Step into a right lunge punch.

4. Move your weight over the left foot and pull the front foot back. Prepare for a right down block.

5. Slide the right foot and turn into a right down block.

6. Step into a left lunge punch.

7. Pull the front (left) foot and hand back while pivoting ninety degrees to the left. Prepare for a left down block.

8. Push the left foot forward into a left down block.

9. Step forward into a right lunge punch.

10. Step forward into a left lunge punch.

11. Step forward into a right lunge punch. Shout *"KI-AI."*

12. Prepare for a left down block by turning the body counterclockwise, pivoting on the heel of the right foot.

13. Turn into a left down block.

SPARRING
(kumite)

Sparring is practicing karate techniques with a partner. You must control your techniques and your emotions to avoid injuring your partner. Sparring is good preparation for sport karate. Light contact is made in sport karate, but hitting an opponent hard will lead to disqualification. Sport karate requires fast reflexes, good timing, and an understanding of the correct distance for each technique.

BLOCK AND COUNTER TO HEAD PUNCH

1. Attacker is in basic ready stance. Defender is ready to block.

BLOCK AND COUNTER TO BODY PUNCH

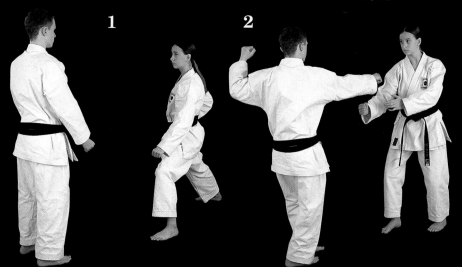

1. Attacker is in basic ready stance. Defender is ready to block.

2. Attacker steps forward to punch. Defender moves backward to block.

A strong "ki-ai" shows a good fighting spirit.

BLOCK AND COUNTER TO HEAD KICK

1. Attacker and defender face each other in front stances.

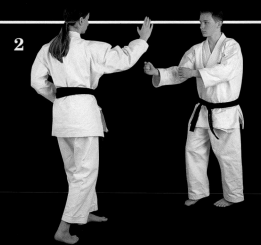

2. Attacker steps forward to punch. Defender moves backward to block.

3. Attacker punches to the head. Defender performs a rising block.

4. Defender counterattacks with a reverse punch to the body.

3. Attacker punches to the body. Defender performs an outside block.

4. Defender counterattacks with a reverse punch to the head.

The fighter on the right moves inside the kick to counterattack his opponent.

2. Attacker performs a roundhouse kick to the head. Defender blocks with both hands.

3. Defender counterattacks with a roundhouse kick to the body.

SELF-DEFENSE TECHNIQUES
(goshin jutsu)

The most traditional use of karate is in self-defense against an attacker. You should use only as much force as is necessary to stop an attacker from hurting you.

DEFENSE AGAINST A LAPEL GRAB

1. Attacker grabs your lapels.

2. Step back and force the attacker's arms apart. Stepping back causes the attacker to lose his or her balance.

3. Counterattack by driving the knee of your rear leg into your attacker's stomach or groin.

Pulling the attacker into the counterattack maximizes the effect of the blow. This technique is dangerous. It should be used only when no other choice is available.

DEFENSE AGAINST A HOOK PUNCH

1   **2**   **3**   **4**

1. Attacker punches at your head with a right hook.

2. Step away from the punch slightly, blocking it with your left forearm.

3. Wrap your left arm around the attacker's right arm and apply force* to the elbow joint.

Do not apply force when practicing with a partner.

4. Counterattack with a palm heel strike to the chin.

A palm heel strike should use enough force to drive the attacker's head backward, stunning the attacker and forcing him or her off balance.

WARNING!
All self-defense techniques are dangerous. Do not practice them at all until you have developed good control of your techniques. Do not practice them with a partner unless you are supervised by your instructor or a senior student.

USEFUL INFORMATION

There are many karate organizations that promote and teach traditional karate and related martial arts. Use the resources on this page to find information on the locations of schools and clubs, training methods, and styles.

Shotokan Karate of America
www.ska.org

USA Karate Federation
www.usakarate.org

USA National Karate-do Federation
www.usankf.org

All of the Internet addresses (URLs) given in this book were valid at the time of going to press. Due to the dynamic nature of the Internet, however, some addresses may have changed, or sites may have ceased to exist since publication. While the author and publishers regret any inconvenience to readers, they can accept no responsibility for any Internet changes.

Useful addresses:
Shotokan Karate of America
222 S. Hewitt Street, Room 7
Los Angeles, CA 90012
(213) 437-0988

USA Karate Federation
1300 Kenmore Blvd.
Akron, OH 44314
(330) 753-3114

USA National Karate-do Federation
P.O. Box 77083
Seattle, WA 98177-7083
(206) 839-4140

KARATE TERMS

age empi: rising elbow strike

age uke: rising block

choku zuki: standing punch

dan: karate grades at black belt level and above

dojo: martial arts training hall

empi: elbow

fundoshi: loincloth

gedan barai: down block, lower sweeping block

Goju Ryu: name of a karate style, literally "hard and soft"

goshin jutsu: self-defense techniques

gyaku zuki: reverse punch

hiji: elbow

karate: "empty hand" (originally "China hand")

kata: forms

ki-ai: karate shout

kiba dachi: straddle stance

kihon: karate basics

kizami zuki: jab punch

kokutsu dachi: back stance

kumite: sparring

kyu: karate grades below black belt

mae geri: front kick

mawashi geri: roundhouse kick

oi zuki: lunge punch

Shito Ryu: name of a karate style

Shotokan: name of a karate style, literally "Shoto's Hall"

shuto uke: knifehand block

sokuto: foot

soto uke: outside block

tachi: stances

Taikyoku: early name for *kihon kata,* literally "Great Ultimate"

uchi uke: inside block

uraken: back fist

ushiro empi: rear elbow strike

ushiro geri: back kick

Wado Ryu: name of a karate style, literally "the Way of Peace"

yoko empi: side elbow strike

yoko geri: side kick

yoko geri keage: side snap kick

yoko geri kekomi: side thrust kick

zenkutsu dachi: front stance

INDEX